P9-CJG-265

A Dream of Summer

Poems for the Sensuous Season

Selected by Robert Atwan

Introduction by Mary Oliver

Beacon Press · Boston

BEACON PRESS
25 Beacon Street
Boston, Massachusetts 02108–2892
www.beacon.org

Beacon Press books are published under the auspices of
the Unitarian Universalist Association of Congregations.

© 2004 by Beacon Press
Introduction copyright © 2004 by Mary Oliver
ALL RIGHTS RESERVED
Printed in the United States of America

14 13 12 11 10   8 7 6 5 4 3 2

This book is printed on acid-free paper that meets the uncoated
paper ANSI/ NISO specifications for permanence as revised in 1992.

Text design by Christopher Kuntze.

LIBRARY OF CONGRESS CATALOGING-IN-PUBLICATION DATA

A dream of summer : poems for the sensuous season / selected by Robert Atwan ;
introduction by Mary Oliver.
        p. cm.
    Includes bibliographical references.
    ISBN 978–0–8070–6872–4 (alk. paper)
    1. Summer—poetry. 2. American poetry. 3. English poetry.   I. Atwan, Robert.
    PS595.S85D74 2004
    811.008'033—dc22   2004000709

CONTENTS

The Beautiful Cloudy Stuff of Dreams

Yes, in summer we all live in the dreamy palace. Let us begin by saying that summer is lavish, fragrant, colorful, slow, humid, calm, or, on occasions, filled with the wild wires of lightning and the great punches that follow; it is fruitful, insectful; the hay is making and the sneezing is becoming universal; all this is commonly true. There are satisfactions beyond number; fishermen get their catch, the food is delicious and real, the sail has just enough wind; the children, in the country at least, play riotously and can hardly be persuaded to remember the necessity of sleep, even when the fireflies are blinking as high as their bedroom windows. Also, the heat makes of neighborhood a genuine thing, people are out on lawns or porches; they are exhausted, happy, beneficent, less ambitious than in any other season, and they are full of the beautiful cloudy stuff of dreams.

So the poets, in this fullness, write of the wonder of the experience, the touch and the taste, the tenderness of the earth clothed in leaves and flowers, and the tenderness too of love, grown from the stinging desires of spring to the intimate agreements of summer. Says May Sarton, "It is lulling and so mild." And later, it is "golden-buttercup-wild." Thoreau speaks of the "visible heat." A house becomes "a lilting house" and a young boy turns "green and golden," says Dylan Thomas. "The poetry of earth is never dead," says Keats. But this is later, past the end of the golden season, and it is both affirmation and, in a way, protest. Which, every year, as summer wanes, we must come to.

There is a dark window through which every summer drains away, and poets will speak of that also, a meditation on time and change. The truth is, if summer continued forever, it would be less lovely. We are fickle; we value in spite of ourselves the smart of uncertain hope, the mixture of events and the seasons; we have a liking for change as for condiments and love to taste their might; we see within every delight the seed that has opened and bloomed and now offers wilt, and what are you going to say about that?

Take Frost. Frost is a magical poet—how his music flows, riparian and silky, while the truth, sometimes the low-hearted truth, strikes its sparks in an almost unnoticed minor key. Summer is "a diminished thing," sings his ovenbird. And not a syllable of the poet's commentary protesting? What happened to fullness, glory, all that green plenty? What happened, as a matter of fact, to the birds? Well, Frost is right, they are in spring wild to claim territory, to charm the ladies; full-throated they lean out of the leaves above us, on every path, and sing, though not to us. But now, in the heavy heat, in the task of feeding the young ones, they sit in the best shade they can find, and their little beaks open more and more silently. Frost dares to say it, or rather to suggest it through his interpretation of the ovenbird, that ground-loving warbler, a rare one, that sings all through the summer.

But look! The roses are in full bloom. The morning glories can climb no higher. The corn is on its way to a rich harvest. The farmer looks lovingly at his fields. The beloved looks at his or her beloved, lovingly. The child gathers fireflies, the corn fattens, love becomes a household of children. Spring is a rising. Summer is a season; it almost seems sometimes, in the beautiful, dusty hours, that time is not moving at all.

One day a friend, a physical oceanographer, was watching from our front window the high tide moving in. I expressed some concern, seeing how close it was coming already to the neighbor's deck, and ours too, with a good half hour for the water to splash in, before the moment of high tide. Our friend drew a line across the newspaper he was holding, an undulating line with four peaks and four valleys, then two additional lines touching the peaks and the deepest area of descent. And he explained the energy of the motions up and down the sides of the curves, and the diminished energy at the top and the bottom. Say, for example, at high tide or at low tide. It's now the period of high tide, he said, and the water won't climb much more, the houses are safe. And I thought of spring flashing forth and hurrying through the rain, and of autumn flashing forth and down, to the slow, slow winter. And I thought of Robley Wilson saying, "In summer, nothing happens." Or so it seems, in that world stitched together flower by flower, bean by bean.

But, of course there is important work being done, by every living spirit, while the beans swell and the roots of the flowers grow strong in the sweet-smelling earth. It is called idling. Whitman was probably the best idler any of us has ever met. By idling I don't mean resting, neither do I mean doing nothing. I mean Whitman's kind of muscleless stance, as all his senses, his eyes, ears, his tongue, and his heart take in the sensuous gifts of the season. It is from such attention that happiness comes, and the imagination blooms forth with the most exquisite words. Be they simple or complex. Robert Hayden, in the heat-heavy ghetto, cries out "Oh, summer, summer summertime," then ends with "big/splendiferous/ Jack Johnson in his diamond limousine/set the ghetto burgeoning/with fantasies/of Ethiopia spreading her gorgeous wings." Country or city, summer is the throne room of the spirit, and of the poet, the tongue wanting the taste of the leaves, and the taste of the words to tell the taste of the leaves.

Such is the power of Logos, when the heart is full. Reading this collection is visiting summer, even if the snow is falling fast just beyond the window. You will still see the bobolink, and the green corn, and the red rose, and the lover hoping his beloved will come. There is, at the end of a Willa Cather story, this simple sentence: "The roses of song and the roses of memory, they are the only ones that last."

A Dream of Summer

Summer Music

Summer is all a green air—
From the brilliant lawn, sopranos
Through murmuring hedges
Accompanied by some poplars;
In fields of wheat, surprises;
Through faraway pastures, flows
To the horizon's blues
In slow decrescendos.

Summer is all a green sound—
Rippling in the foreground
To that soft applause,
The foam of Queen Anne's lace.
Green, green in the ear
Is all we care to hear—
Until a field suddenly flashes
The singing with so sharp
A yellow that it crashes
Loud cymbals in the ear,
Minor has turned to major
As summer, lulling and so mild,
Goes golden-buttercup-wild.

Solstice

Each year, on this same date, the summer solstice comes.
Consummate light: we plan for it,
the day we tell ourselves
that time is very long indeed, nearly infinite.
And in our reading and writing, preference is given
to the celebratory, the ecstatic.

There is in these rituals something apart from wonder:
there is also a kind of preening,
as though human genius had participated in these arrangements
and we found the results satisfying.

What follows the light is what precedes it:
the moment of balance, of dark equivalence.

But tonight we sit in the garden in our canvas chairs
so late into the evening—
why should we look either forward or backward?
Why should we be forced to remember:
it is in our blood, this knowledge.
Shortness of the days; darkness, coldness of winter.
It is in our blood and bones; it is in our history.
It takes genius to forget these things.

June Bracken and Heather

To ———————

There on the top of the down,
The wild heather round me and over me June's high blue,
When I looked at the bracken so bright and the heather so
    brown,
I thought to myself I would offer this book to you,
This, and my love together,
To you that are seventy-seven,
With a faith as clear as the heights of the June-blue heaven,
And a fancy as summer-new
As the green of the bracken amid the gloom of the heather.

Pear Tree

Silver dust,
lifted from the earth,
higher than my arms reach,
you have mounted,
O, silver,
higher than my arms reach,
you front us with great mass;

no flower ever opened
so staunch a white leaf,
no flower ever parted silver
from such rare silver;

O, white pear,
your flower-tufts
thick on the branch
bring summer and ripe fruits
in their purple hearts.

Days

Daughters of Time, the hypocritic Days,
Muffled and dumb like barefoot dervishes,
And marching single in an endless file,
Bring diadems and fagots in their hands.
To each they offer gifts after his will,
Bread, kingdoms, stars, and sky that holds them all.
I, in my pleachèd garden, watched the pomp,
Forgot my morning wishes, hastily
Took a few herbs and apples, and the Day
Turned and departed silent. I, too late,
Under her solemn fillet saw the scorn.

While I Am Writing a Poem to Celebrate Summer, the Meadowlark Begins to Sing

Sixty-seven years, oh Lord, to look at the clouds,
the trees in deep, moist summer,

daisies and morning glories
opening every morning

their small, ecstatic faces—
Or maybe I should just say

How I wish I had a voice
like the meadowlark's,

sweet, clear, and reliably
slurring all day long

from the fencepost, or the long grass
where it lives

in a tiny but adequate grass hut
beside the mullein and the everlasting,

the faint-pink roses
that have never been improved, but come to bud

then open like little soft sighs
under the meadowlark's whistle, its breath-praise,

its thrill-song, its anthem, its thanks, its
alleluia. Alleluia, oh Lord.

Woof of the Sun, Ethereal Gauze

Woof of the sun, ethereal gauze,
Woven of Nature's richest stuffs,
Visible heat, air-water, and dry sea,
Last conquest of the eye;
Toil of the day displayed, sun-dust,
Aerial surf upon the shores of earth,
Ethereal estuary, frith of light,
Breakers of air, billows of heat,
Fine summer spray on inland seas;
Bird of the sun, transparent-winged
Owlet of noon, soft-pinioned,
From heath or stubble rising without song;
Establish thy serenity o'er the fields.

Shall I Compare Thee to a Summer's Day?

Shall I compare thee to a summer's day?
Thou art more lovely and more temperate.
Rough winds do shake the darling buds of May,
And summer's lease hath all too short a date.
Sometime too hot the eye of heaven shines,
And often is his gold complexion dimmed;
And every fair from fair sometime declines,
By chance, or nature's changing course, untrimmed;
But thy eternal summer shall not fade,
Nor lose possession of that fair thou ow'st,
Nor shall death brag thou wand'rest in his shade,
When in eternal lines to Time thou grow'st.
　　So long as men can breathe, or eyes can see,
　　So long lives this, and this gives life to thee.

Childhood

Summer brought fireflies in swarms.
They lit our evenings like dreams
we thought we couldn't have.
We caught them in jars, punched
holes, carried them around for days.

Luminous abdomens that when charged
with air turned bright. Imagine!
mere insects carrying such cargo,
magical caravans flickering beneath
low July skies. We chased them, amazed.

The idea! Those tiny bodies
pulsing phosphorescence.
They made reckless traffic,
signaling, neon flashes forever
into the deepening dusk.

They gave us new faith
in the nasty tonics of childhood,
pungent, murky liquids promising
shining eyes, strong teeth, glowing skin,
and we silently vowed to swallow ever after.

What was the secret of light?
We wanted their brilliance:
small fires hovering,
each tiny explosion
the birth of a new world.

ELIZABETH JENNINGS

An English Summer

An English summer—and a sense of form
Rides the five senses that dispute their claims.
Lawns leveled against nature, airs which warm
Each plant, perpetuate the hours and names.
We cannot see beyond the blue; no storm
Vies with the children ardent at their games.

Childhood returns with summer. It is strange
That such a season brings one's memories back.
Springs have their homesickness, autumns arrange
The sweet nostalgias that we long to lack.
But summer is itself; it's we who change
And lay our childhoods on the golden stack.

My fingers rest and eyes concern their sight
Simply with what would live were I not here.
It is the concentration of the light
That shows the other side of pain and fear.
I watch, incredulous of such delight,
Wanting the meaning not the landscape clear.

Was it for this the breath once breathed upon
The waters that we rose from? I can see
Only a summer with its shadows gone,
Skies that refuse an alien dignity.
But gardens, gardens echo. What sun shone
To make this truce with pain and ecstasy?

DYLAN THOMAS

Fern Hill

Now as I was young and easy under the apple boughs
About the lilting house and happy as the grass was green,
    The night above the dingle starry,
        Time let me hail and climb
      Golden in the heydays of his eyes,
And honoured among wagons I was prince of the apple towns
And once below a time I lordly had the trees and leaves
      Trail with daisies and barley
    Down the rivers of the windfall light.

And as I was green and carefree, famous among the barns
  About the happy yard and singing as the farm was home,
    In the sun that is young once only,
        Time let me play and be
      Golden in the mercy of his means,
And green and golden I was huntsman and herdsman, the calves
Sang to my horn, the foxes on the hills barked clear and cold,
      And the sabbath rang slowly
    In the pebbles of the holy streams.

All the sun long it was running, it was lovely, the hay
Fields high as the house, the tunes from the chimneys, it was air
    And playing, lovely and watery
      And fire green as grass.
    And nightly under the simple stars

As I rode to sleep the owls were bearing the farm away,
All the moon long I heard, blessed among stables, the night-jars
    Flying with the ricks, and the horses
        Flashing into the dark.

And then to awake, and the farm, like a wanderer white
With the dew, come back, the cock on his shoulder: it was all
    Shining, it was Adam and maiden,
        The sky gathered again
        And the sun grew round that very day.
So it must have been after the birth of the simple light
In the first, spinning place, the spellbound horses walking warm
    Out of the whinnying green stable
        On to the fields of praise.

And honoured among foxes and pheasants by the gay house
Under the new made clouds and happy as the heart was long,
    In the sun born over and over,
        I ran my heedless ways,
    My wishes raced through the house high hay
And nothing I cared, at my sky blue trades, that time allows
In all his tuneful turning so few and such morning songs
    Before the children green and golden
        Follow him out of grace,

Nothing I cared, in the lamb white days, that time would take me
Up to the swallow thronged loft by the shadow of my hand,
   In the moon that is always rising,
      Nor that riding to sleep
   I should hear him fly with the high fields
And wake to the farm forever fled from the childless land.
Oh as I was young and easy in the mercy of his means,
   Time held me green and dying
      Though I sang in my chains like the sea.

CAROLYN MILLER

Dark, Starry, Sticky Night: Missouri

It's like falling into warm molasses, a dark
sweetness in which you can barely breathe; it's like
being drowned in blackness, thick and moving
in slow waves around you, while above you shine the steady
lights of stars, and around you flicker the floating,
intermittent lights of lightning bugs; the smell of flowers
grows even stronger on the warm tide of the night,
all of summer welling into a flood of fragrance and
a heavy mixture of sex and sorrow, and everywhere
cicadas and crickets are rasping out their brief sentient lives,
and off in the woods a whippoorwill keeps calling
that each moment is sweeter and more precious
than any you will ever taste again.

A July Afternoon by the Pond

The fervent heat, but so much more endurable in this pure
air—the white and pink pond-blossoms, with great heart-
shaped leaves; the glassy waters of the creek, the banks,
with dense bushery, and the picturesque beeches and shade
and turf; the tremulous, reedy call of some bird from
recesses, breaking the warm, indolent, half-voluptuous
silence; an occasional wasp, hornet, honey-bee or bumble
(they hover near my hands or face, yet annoy me not, nor I
them, as they appear to examine, find nothing, and away
they go)—the vast space of the sky overhead so clear, and
the buzzard up there sailing his slow whirl in majestic spi-
rals and discs; just over the surface of the pond, two large
slate-color'd dragon-flies, with wings of lace, circling and
darting and occasionally balancing themselves quite still,
their wings quivering all the time, (are they not showing off
for my amusement?)—the pond itself, with the sword-
shaped calamus; the water snakes—occasionally a flitting
blackbird, with red dabs on his shoulders, as he darts slant-
ingly by—the sounds that bring out the solitude, warmth,
light and shade—the quawk of some pond duck—(the
crickets and grasshoppers are mute in the noon heat, but I
hear the song of the first cicadas;)—then at some distance
the rattle and whirr of a reaping machine as the horses
draw it on a rapid walk through a rye field on the opposite
side of the creek—(what was the yellow or light-brown

bird, large as a young hen, with short neck and long-stretch'd legs I just saw, in flapping and awkward flight over there through the trees?)—the prevailing delicate, yet palpable, spicy, grassy, clovery perfume to my nostrils; and over all, encircling all, to my sight and soul, the free space of the sky, transparent and blue—and hovering there in the west, a mass of white-gray fleecy clouds the sailors call "shoals of mackerel"—the sky, with silver swirls like locks of toss'd hair, spreading, expanding—a vast voiceless, form-less simulacrum—yet may-be the most real reality and for-mulator of everything—who knows?

ROBLEY WILSON

In summer, nothing happens

In summer, nothing happens.
The girls one hungers to love
have taken jobs by the sea,
the friends one banters with
are hauling Airstream trailers
westward into the mountains.
The neighbors have left only
their frantic dogs—boys
no one has seen before
come to scour the kennels.
A stranger on a riding mower
does all the lawns together.

What is the change in summer
of which one expects nothing?
Nature is not reborn,
nor does she perish except
in the streaks of a rare elm
that has outlived itself.
The weather conceals nothing:
the months are temperate,
even in the hardest rains
one may walk without a coat.
The gardens flourish, and bear
without a gardener's help.

Sitting in windows at night
black cats and their masters
look out on summer; the moon
feeds their yellow visions,
the opened windows cool them.
One learns to smoke a pipe
and is pleased for solitude.
One wants nothing to happen
forever, and thinks of those
who perhaps are ready to die,
except that it is summer
and they are putting it off.

Gic to Har

It is late at night, cold and damp
The air is filled with tobacco smoke.
My brain is worried and tired.
I pick up the encyclopedia,
The volume GIC to HAR,
It seems I have read everything in it,
So many other nights like this.
I sit staring empty-headed at the article Grosbeak,
Listening to the long rattle and pound
Of freight cars and switch engines in the distance.
Suddenly I remember
Coming home from swimming
In Ten Mile Creek,
Over the long moraine in the early summer evening,
My hair wet, smelling of waterweeds and mud.
I remember a sycamore in front of a ruined farmhouse,
And instantly and clearly the revelation
Of a song of incredible purity and joy,
My first rose-breasted grosbeak,
Facing the low sun, his body
Suffused with light.
I was motionless and cold in the hot evening
Until he flew away, and I went on knowing
In my twelfth year one of the great things
Of my life had happened.

Thirty factories empty their refuse in the creek.
On the parched lawns are starlings, alien and aggressive.
And I am on the other side of the continent
Ten years in an unfriendly city.

Sleep in Summer

Light wakes us—there's the sun
climbing the mountains' rim, spilling across the valley,
finding our faces.
It is July,
        between the hay and harvest,
a time at arm's length from all other time,
the roads ragged with meadowsweet and mallow,
with splays of seedheads, slubbed and coarse, rough linen.
The fields above the house, clotted with sheep all spring,
are empty now and froth with flowering grasses,
still in the morning light. Birds move around
the leafy fields, the leafy garden.

It is the time
to set aside all vigil, good or ill,
to loosen the fixed gaze of our attention
as dandelions let seedlings to the wind.
Wake with the light.
Get up and go about the day and watch
its surfaces that brighten with the sun.
Remark the weight of your hands,
your foot in its sandal,
the lavender's blue hum.

And later, when the light is drowsed and heavy
go find the burdened fruit trees where the shade
lies splashed and opened-out across the ground.
Spread over it a quilt worn soft by other bodies,
then curl and fall down into sleep in light.

Awaken to a world of long, loose grass-stems,
and leaves above,
and birds, breaking out of the leaves.

Summer

There is that sound like the wind
Forgetting in the branches that means something
Nobody can translate. And there is the sobering "later on,"
When you consider what a thing meant, and put it down.

For the time being the shadow is ample
And hardly seen, divided among the twigs of a tree,
The trees of a forest, just as life is divided up
Between you and me, and among all the others out there.

And the thinning-out phase follows
The period of reflection. And suddenly, to be dying
Is not a little or mean or cheap thing,
Only wearying, the heat unbearable,

And also the little mindless constructions put upon
Our fantasies of what we did: summer, the ball of pine needles,
The loose fates serving our acts, with token smiles,
Carrying out their instructions too accurately—

Too late to cancel them now—and winter, the twitter
Of cold stars at the pane, that describes with broad gestures
This state of being that is not so big after all.
Summer involves going down as a steep flight of steps

To a narrow ledge over the water. Is this it, then,
This iron comfort, these reasonable taboos,
Or did you mean it when you stopped? And the face
Resembles yours, the one reflected in the water.

Dark Summer

Under the thunder-dark, the cicadas resound.
The storm in the sky mounts, but is not yet heard.
The shaft and the flash wait, but are not yet found.

The apples that hang and swell for the late comer,
The simple spell, the rite not for our word,
The kisses not for our mouths,—light the dark summer.

My Father Paints the Summer

A smoky rain riddles the ocean plains,
Rings on the beaches' stones, stomps in the swales,
Batters the panes
Of the shore hotel, and the hoped-for summer chills and fails.
The summer people sigh,
"Is this July?"

They talk by the lobby fire but no one hears
For the thrum of the rain. In the dim and sounding halls,
Din at the ears,
Dark at the eyes well in the head, and the ping-pong balls
Scatter their hollow knocks
Like crazy clocks.

But up in his room by artificial light
My father paints the summer, and his brush
Tricks into sight
The prosperous sleep, the girdling stir and clear steep hush
Of a summer never seen,
A granted green.

Summer, luxuriant Sahara, the orchard spray
Gales in the Eden trees, the knight again
Can cast away

His burning mail, Rome is at Anzio: but the rain
For the ping-pong's optative bop
Will never stop.

Caught Summer is always an imagined time.
Time gave it, yes, but time out of any mind.
There must be prime
In the heart to beget that season, to reach past rain and find
Riding the palest days
Its perfect blaze.

THOMAS HARDY

At the Royal Academy

These summer landscapes—clump, and copse, and croft—
Woodland and meadowland—here hung aloft,
Gay with limp grass and leafery new and soft,

Seem caught from the immediate season's yield
I saw last noonday shining over the field,
By rapid snatch, while still are uncongealed

The saps that in their live originals climb;
Yester's quick greenage here set forth in mime
Just as it stands, now, at our breathing-time.

But these young foils so fresh upon each tree,
Soft verdures spread in sprouting novelty,
Are not this summer's though they feign to be.

Last year their May to Michaelmas term was run,
Last autumn browned and buried every one,
And no more know they sight of any sun.

The House Was Quiet and the World Was Calm

The house was quiet and the world was calm.
The reader became the book; and summer night

Was like the conscious being of the book.
The house was quiet and the world was calm.

The words were spoken as if there was no book,
Except that the reader leaned above the page,

Wanted to lean, wanted much most to be
The scholar to whom his book is true, to whom

The summer night is like a perfection of thought.
The house was quiet because it had to be.

The quiet was part of the meaning, part of the mind:
The access of perfection to the page.

And the world was calm. The truth in a calm world,
In which there is no other meaning, itself

Is calm, itself is summer and night, itself
Is the reader leaning late and reading there.

Happiness

Snaked through oaks, wild fruit
& honeysuckle. Baskets overflowed
The bank. Big boys whistled at girls
& swandived from the tallest trees.
Small boys on the plankwalk
Jostled each other, springing up
& down like pogo sticks.
I turned the handle faster,
But the goat in the tree
Remained: Daddy Red forced
Me to stroke the throat
Before his butcher knife
Caught the sunlight.
The cry was a child's.
Silence belonged to gods.
There was no paradise, no
Cakewalk for demons hidden
In grass. Old Lazy Bones
Shook out his limbs & pinwheeled
A dustdevil's foxtrot. The air
Sweetened with the scent of goat
Cooking over a pit,
& as the icecream hardened
The hurt in my arms
Made me happy.

ANNE SEXTON

The Kite

West Harwich, Massachusetts, 1954–1959

Here, in front of the summer hotel
the beach waits like an altar.
We are lying on a cloth of sand
while the Atlantic noon stains
the world in light.

                   It was much the same
five years ago. I remember
how Ezio Pinza was flying a kite
for the children. None of us noticed
it then. The pleated lady
was still a nest of her knitting.
Four pouchy fellows kept their policy
of gin and tonic while trading some money.
The parasol girls slept, sun-sitting
their lovely years. No one thought
how precious it was, or even how funny
the festival seemed, square rigged in the air.
The air was a season they had bought,
like the cloth of sand.

                  I've been waiting
on this private stretch of summer land,
counting these five years and wondering why.

I mean, it was different that time
with Ezio Pinza flying a kite.
Maybe, after all, he knew something more
and was right.

Bleecker Street, Summer

Summer for prose and lemons, for nakedness and languor,
for the eternal idleness of the imagined return,
for rare flutes and bare feet, and the August bedroom
of tangled sheets and the Sunday salt, ah violin!

When I press summer dusks together, it is
a month of street accordions and sprinklers
laying the dust, small shadows running from me.

It is music opening and closing, *Italia mia*, on Bleecker,
ciao, Antonio, and the water-cries of children
tearing the rose-coloured sky in streams of paper;
it is dusk in the nostrils and the smell of water
down littered streets that lead you to no water,
and gathering islands and lemons in the mind.

There is the Hudson, like the sea aflame.
I would undress you in the summer heat,
and laugh and dry your damp flesh if you came.

"Summertime and the Living ..."

Nobody planted roses, he recalls,
but sunflowers gangled there sometimes,
tough-stalked and bold
and like the vivid children there unplanned.
There circus-poster horses curveted
in trees of heaven
above the quarrels and shattered glass,
and he was bareback rider of them all.

No roses there in summer—
oh, never roses except when people died—
and no vacations for his elders,
so harshened after each unrelenting day
that they were shouting-angry.
But summer was, they said, the poor folks' time
of year. And he remembers
how they would sit on broken steps amid

The fevered tossings of the dusk, the dark,
wafting hearsay with funeral-parlor fans
or making evening solemn by
their quietness. Feels their Mosaic eyes
upon him, though the florist roses
that only sorrow could afford
long since have bidden them Godspeed.

Oh, summer summer summertime—
Then grim street preachers shook
their tambourines and Bibles in the face
of tolerant wickedness;
then Elks parades and big splendiferous
Jack Johnson in his diamond limousine
set the ghetto burgeoning
with fantasies
of Ethiopia spreading her gorgeous wings.

Very late July

July in the afternoon, the sky
rings, a crystal goblet without a crack.
One gull passes over mewing for company.
A tiger swallowtail hovers near magenta
phlox, while a confetti cloud
of fritillaries covers the goldenglow.
The sun lowers a helmet of flame
over my skull till my brain cooks
yellow as chicken skin. Beside me
half under the tent of my skirt, my cat
blinks at the day, content watching,
allowing the swallowtail to light
within paw reach, purring too softly
to be heard, only the vibration from his
brown chest buzzing into my palm.
Among the scarlet blossoms of the runner
beans twining on their tripods
the hummingbird darts like a jet fighter.
Today in think tanks, the data analysts
not on vacation are playing war games.
A worker is packing plutonium by remote
control into new warheads. An adviser
is telling a president as they golf,
we could win it. July without a crack
as we live inside the great world egg.

Summer Noon: 1941

With visionary care
The mind imagines Hell,
Draws fine the sound of flame
Till one can scarcely tell
The nature, or the name,
Or what the thing is for:
    Past summer bough and cry,
The sky, distended, bare,
Now whispers like a shell
Of the increase of war.

    Thus will man reach an end:
In fear of his own will,
Yet moved where it may tend,
With mind and word grown still.

    The fieldmouse and the hare,
The small snake of the garden,
Whose little muscles harden,
Whose eyes now quickened stare,
Though driven by the sound
—Too small and free to pardon!—
Will repossess this ground.

The Supremes

In Ball's Market after surfing till noon,
We stand in wet trunks, shivering,
As icing dissolves off our sweet rolls
Inside the heat-blued counter oven,
When they appear on his portable TV,
Riding a float of chiffon as frothy
As the peeling curl of a wave.
The parade m. c. talks up their hits
And their new houses outside of Detroit,
And old Ball clicks his tongue.
Gloved up to their elbows, their hands raised
Toward us palm out, they sing,
"Stop! In the Name of Love," and don't stop,
But slip into the lower foreground.

Every day of a summer can turn,
From one moment, into a single day.
I saw Diana Ross in her first film
Play a brief scene by the Pacific—
And that was the summer it brought back.
Mornings we paddled out, the waves
Would be little more than embellishments—
Lathework and spun glass,
Gray-green with cold, but flawless.
When the sun burned through the light fog,

They would warm and swell,
Wind-scaled and ragged,
And radios up and down the beach
Would burst on with her voice.

She must remember that summer
Somewhat differently. And so must the two
Who sang with her in long matching gowns,
Standing a step back on her left and right,
As the camera tracked them
Into our eyes in Ball's Market.
But what could we know, tanned white boys,
Wiping sugar and salt from our mouths,
And leaning forward to feel their song?
Not much, except to feel it
Ravel us up like a wave
In the silk of white water,
Simply, sweetly, repeatedly,
And just as quickly let go.

We didn't stop either, which is how
We vanished, too, parting like spray—
Ball's Market, my friends and I.
Dredgers ruined the waves,
Those continuous dawn perfections,
And Ball sold high to the high rises
Cresting over them. His flight out of L.A.,

Heading for Vegas, would have banked
Above the wavering lines of surf.
He may have seen them. I have,
Leaving again for points north and east,
Glancing down as the plane turns.
From that height they still look frail and frozen,
Full of simple sweetness and repetition.

The Oven Bird

There is a singer everyone has heard,
Loud, a mid-summer and a mid-wood bird,
Who makes the solid tree trunks sound again.
He says that leaves are old and that for flowers
Mid-summer is to spring as one to ten.
He says the early petal-fall is past
When pear and cherry bloom went down in showers
On sunny days a moment overcast;
And comes that other fall we name the fall.
He says the highway dust is over all.
The bird would cease and be as other birds
But that he knows in singing not to sing.
The question that he frames in all but words
Is what to make of a diminished thing.

A. R. AMMONS

Mid-August

Now the ridge
brooks
are
flue-dry, the rocks

parching hot &
where sluice
used
to clear roots &

break weeds down brambly,
light finds a luminous
sand-scar,
vertical: it will

go to a hundred
today: even the
zucchini vine has
rolled over

on its
side.

RICHARD EBERHART

A Loon Call

Rowing between Pond and Western Islands
As the tide was coming in
Creating, for so long, two barred islands,
At the end of August, fall nip in the air,
I sensed something beyond me,
Everywhere I felt it in my flesh
As I beheld the sea and sky, the day,
The wordless immanence of the eternal,
And as I was rowing backward
To see directly where I was going,
Harmonious in the freedom of the oars,
A solitary loon cry locked the waters.

Barbaric, indivisible, replete with rack,
Somewhere off where seals were on half-tide rocks,
A loon's cry from beyond the human
Shook my sense to wordlessness.

Perfect cry, ununderstandable essence
Of sound from aeons ago, a shriek,
Strange, palpable, ebullient, wavering,
A cry that I cannot understand.
Praise to the cry that I cannot understand.

End of Summer

An agitation of the air,
A perturbation of the light
Admonished me the unloved year
Would turn on its hinge that night.

I stood in the disenchanted field
Amid the stubble and the stones,
Amazed, while a small worm lisped to me
The song of my marrow-bones.

Blue poured into summer blue,
A hawk broke from his cloudless tower,
The roof of the silo blazed, and I knew
That part of my life was over.

Already the iron door of the north
Clangs open: birds, leaves, snows
Order their populations forth,
And a cruel wind blows.

Mother, Summer, I

My mother, who hates thunderstorms,
Holds up each summer day and shakes
It out suspiciously, lest swarms
Of grape-dark clouds are lurking there;
But when the August weather breaks
And rains begin, and brittle frost
Sharpens the bird-abandoned air,
Her worried summer look is lost.

And I her son, though summer-born
And summer-loving, none the less
Am easier when the leaves are gone;
Too often summer days appear
Emblems of perfect happiness
I can't confront: I must await
A time less bold, less rich, less clear:
An autumn more appropriate.

Surface Effects in Summer Wind

I'm learning to remember the sound
days make: one sky disdaining the idea
of clouds, sunlight surviving
its centrifuge, breeze keeping blessed September
at bay. Sweet smell of short-haired boys
I try to recall, having been away from skin
for so long, some youth theirs or mine,
sprint for shelter from an August
one o'clock, heat's peak: season's
entourage with a line of sweat
kissing the shirt to the chest, a valor.
I could believe the earth itself
thought well of those domesticated
demigods, adhering to new
sidewalks in several likenesses.
So walked beside water instead.
(Dear echo, lake, repeating
wake where I find my face awash
in rocks and algae, stuttered counterpoint
of surge and current.) Midnight,
look at the things I've done
in your name, in my dark, walking out
into the street that changes nothing, littered

with leaves and cellophane, giving a little light
back, giving it away. The promised pleasure
locked in a stranger's careless body, his smell
in morning sheets; a jump of cards
in an idle man's hands, and summer ends.

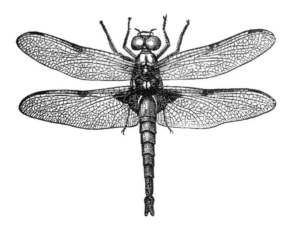

Exeunt

Piecemeal the summer dies;
At the field's edge a daisy lives alone;
A last shawl of burning lies
On a gray field-stone.

All cries are thin and terse;
The field has droned the summer's final mass;
A cricket like a dwindled hearse
Crawls from the dry grass.

EMILY DICKINSON

Further in Summer than the Birds

Further in Summer than the Birds
Pathetic from the Grass
A minor Nation celebrates
Its unobtrusive Mass.

No Ordinance be seen
So gradual the Grace
A pensive Custom it becomes
Enlarging Loneliness.

Antiquest felt at Noon
When August burning low
Arise this spectral Canticle
Repose to typify

Remit as yet no Grace
No Furrow on the Glow
Yet a Druidic Difference
Enhances Nature now

On the Grasshopper and the Cricket

The poetry of earth is never dead:
　　When all the birds are faint with the hot sun,
　　And hide in cooling trees, a voice will run
From hedge to hedge about the new-mown mead;
That is the Grasshopper's—he takes the lead
　　In summer luxury,—he has never done
　　With his delights; for when tired out with fun
He rests at ease beneath some pleasant weed.
The poetry of earth is ceasing never:
　　On a lone winter evening, when the frost
　　　　Has wrought a silence, from the stove there shrills
The Cricket's song, in warmth increasing ever,
　　And seems to one in drowsiness half lost,
　　　　The Grasshopper's among some grassy hills.

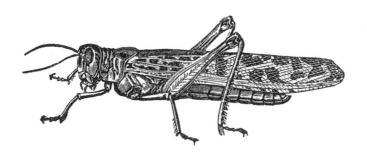

BIOGRAPHICAL NOTES BY ROBERT ATWAN

Although he wrote poems on just about every topic under the sun, A(rchibald) R(andolph) **Ammons** (1926–2001) was especially sensitive to the outdoor world—the seasons, the weather, the woods, the endless varieties of sky above. His keen love of nature is reflected in many of the titles he gave his collections: *Expressions of Sea Level* (1964), *Uplands* (1970), *The Snow Poems* (1977), *A Coast of Trees* (1981), and *Lake-Effect Country* (1983). Raised on a North Carolina farm, Ammons graduated from Wake Forest University with a degree in science. The recipient of numerous awards, including two National Book Awards and a MacArthur Fellowship, Ammons taught at Cornell University from 1964 until his retirement in 1998.

With their free-floating referents, unsupplied contexts, and labyrinthine visual patterns, **John Ashbery**'s poems seem to welcome misreadings and compel rereadings. The literary successor of Wallace Stevens (see below) and, perhaps more important, Gertrude Stein, Ashbery was born on an upstate New York farm in 1927. After graduating from Harvard in 1949, he earned an MA at Columbia and spent a decade in Paris writing art criticism and reviews, an experience that not only helped inform his poetry but led to positions as an art critic back home for *Art News* and *Newsweek*. Selected by W. H. Auden for the prestigious Yale Series of Younger Poets, Ashbery's first book, *Some Trees* (1956), was followed by such challenging volumes as *The Tennis Court Oath* (1962), *Rivers and Mountains* (1966), *The Double Dream of Spring* (1970), and the Pulitzer Prize–winning *Self-Portrait in a Convex Mirror* (1975), all of which put him permanently at the forefront of contemporary American poetry and earned him many distinguished awards, including a MacArthur Fellowship. Ashbery's later works include *Wakefulness* (1998), *Your Name Here* (2000), and *Chinese Whispers* (2002). A former chancellor of the Academy of American Poets, he is the Charles P. Stevenson Jr. Professor of Languages and Literature at Bard College.

A longtime poetry reviewer for the *New Yorker,* **Louise Bogan** (1897–1970) earned a serious reputation as both a critic and a poet. Born in Maine and educated in Boston schools, she married in 1916 and within a few years had a child, separated, and moved to Greenwich Village, where she formed associations with various literary groups and magazines and became one of the earliest Americans to undergo intensive psychoanalytic treatment, which she continued throughout her life. Her collections include *Body of*

This Death (1923), *Dark Summer* (1929), *The Sleeping Fury* (1937), and *The Blue Estuaries: Poems 1923–1968* (1968).

Emily Dickinson (1830–1886) spent practically her entire life as a recluse in her parents' home in Amherst, Massachusetts, where her father served as treasurer of Amherst College. Although she wrote nearly two thousand poems, only a few were published in her lifetime. The first complete and textually authentic collection of her poetry did not appear until 1955, a publishing event that surely qualifies her as one of America's leading "modern" poets. Through uncanny paths of perception and with remarkable compression, her poems, like momentary flashes of insight, take us to the edges of human thought. Yet, as enigmatic as these mental journeys may seem, they are firmly rooted in a particular place: "I see—New Englandly," she once rhymed.

Hilda Doolittle (1886–1961), known throughout her career as H. D., was born into a prominent Bethlehem, Pennsylvania, family. She attended Bryn Mawr briefly, forming friendships with classmate Marianne Moore and University of Pennsylvania student Ezra Pound, with whom she engaged in a complicated romance. In 1911 she moved to London and joined Pound's literary circle. She published her first work in *Poetry* magazine in 1913, the year she married D. H. Lawrence's friend Richard Aldington. She had a daughter with another of Lawrence's friends in 1919, shortly after she met the British literary entrepreneur Winifred Ellerman, who became her lifelong companion and who would later arrange for her psychoanalytic treatment with Sigmund Freud. Such early collections as *Sea Garden* (1916), *The God* (1917), and *Hymen* (1921) entitle H. D. to be remembered as one of the greatest imagist poets, although she had an extraordinarily versatile career, writing some of the earliest articles on cinema (she even starred in a few experimental films) and publishing fiction, essays, several memoirs, and an epic on Helen of Troy, which appeared shortly before her death.

Born into a prominent and prosperous Minnesota family in 1904, **Richard Eberhart** graduated from Dartmouth College in 1926 and did postgraduate work at Cambridge and Harvard. Eberhart worked at many odd jobs, one of them a *King and I* experience as the private tutor to the son of the king of Siam. After naval service during World War II, he worked for several years in his wife's Boston family business but in the early 1950s began a lifetime of teaching at such colleges as Brown, Swarthmore, Tufts, Princeton, and Dartmouth, where he taught from 1956 to 1980. Eberhart published his first book of poetry, *A Bravery of Earth,* in 1931; in 1966 he won a Pulitzer Prize for his *Selected Poems* and in 1977 the National Book

Award for *Collected Poems, 1930–1976*. His *New and Selected Poems* appeared in 1990.

America's greatest essayist and one of its most influential thinkers, **Ralph Waldo Emerson** (1803–1882) eventually persuaded himself that prose—not poetry—was his literary gift. Some of Emerson's finest poems were first written out as prose and later tweaked into verse. Although today his poetry is cited far less frequently than his essays, it has nonetheless attracted many ardent admirers ever since his first volume, *Poems,* appeared in 1847. Robert Frost carried a first edition around with him and knew the poems intimately, considering one of them ("Uriel") "the best Western poem yet." Born in Boston, Emerson moved into his family's home in Concord, Massachusetts, in 1835 and resided there for the remainder of his life.

So closely associated with New England is **Robert Frost** (1874–1963) that few people realize he was actually born in San Francisco. He did not move east until he was eleven, when his father's death left the family penniless. Frost published his first two collections, *A Boy's Will* (1913) and *North of Boston* (1914), in England, where he had gone at thirty-eight to jump-start his career as a poet. "The Oven Bird" appeared in Frost's third poetry volume, *Mountain Interval* (1916), which also featured such enduring poems as "The Road Not Taken," "Birches," and "'Out, Out—'." With this book and the following collection, *New Hampshire* (1923), Frost became the nation's most beloved modern poet, commanding large audiences for his many public readings, the most memorable of which was his recitation of "The Gift Outright" at John F. Kennedy's inauguration in 1961. A sparrow-size forest-floor warbler, the furtive ovenbird is an appropriate Frostian subject; more likely heard than seen. Its distinctive song sounds like *teacher, teacher, teacher, teacher,* gradually increasing in volume.

Louise Glück (pronounced GLICK) was born in New York City in 1943 and attended Sarah Lawrence College and Columbia University's School of General Studies, where she took poetry workshops with Stanley Kunitz (see below). Shortly after the publication of her first volume of poetry, *Firstborn* (1968), she began teaching at Goddard College in Vermont while she self-exorcised the ghosts of the preceding generation of confessional poets in an attempt to develop an original voice confronting new poetic and emotional pressures. The result was her highly acclaimed second volume, *The House on Marshland* (1975), in which she introduced themes she would explore repeatedly in such subsequent books as *Descending Figure* (1980), *The Triumph of Achilles* (1985), *Ararat* (1990), the Pulitzer Prize–winning *The Wild Iris* (1992), and *Meadowlands* (1996). The author of *Proofs and The-*

ories: Essays on Poetry (1994), she taught poetry for many years at Williams College and is now at Yale University. She was appointed U.S. Poet Laureate in 2003. "Solstice" appeared in *The Seven Ages* (2001), one of many poems in that collection that meditates profoundly and elegantly on summer and temporality.

Born in Singapore in 1952, **Kerry Hardie** grew up in County Down, Northern Ireland, studied English at York University, and has worked for both the BBC and the Arts Council of Northern Ireland. She is the author of two volumes of poetry, *A Furious Place* (1996) and *Cry for the Hot Belly* (2000), and a novel, *Hannie Bennet's Winter Marriage* (2000). She shared the Hennessey Award for Poetry in 1995 and the following year won the United Kingdom National Poetry Award. The recipient of the Friends Provident National Poetry Prize, she lives in County Kilkenny, Ireland.

One of the great Victorian novelists, **Thomas Hardy** (1840–1928) stopped writing fiction in 1896 after the hostile reception of *Jude the Obscure* and went on to become one of England's leading poets. Few writers have demonstrated such a mastery of literature's two major genres and had such profound influence on the direction of subsequent fiction and poetry. Born in the rural region near Dorchester in southwest England, which he meticulously remapped as the "Wessex" of his fiction and poetry, Hardy had little formal schooling and at fifteen was apprenticed to an architect, a trade he then practiced in London, where he developed such an interest in reading literature that, upon returning home, he decided to become a writer, publishing twenty novels, including *Far from the Madding Crowd* (1874), *The Return of the Native* (1878), and *Tess of the d'Urbervilles* (1891), before he dedicated himself to the art of poetry with *Wessex Poems* (1898). Although he is best known today for his stern and stoic lyrics, his most ambitious work is his dramatic epic of the Napoleonic Wars, *The Dynasts,* which appeared in three books between 1904 and 1908. Inspired by several realistic summer landscape paintings, "At the Royal Academy" appeared in *Late Lyrics and Earlier* (1922).

Born Asa Bundy Sheffey, **Robert Hayden** (1913–1980) grew up in an impoverished and emotionally turbulent foster family in Detroit and graduated from what is now Wayne State University in 1942, his education interrupted by work researching African American history and culture—a subject that would shape and inform much of his writing—for the Federal Writers' Project. By graduation, Hayden had already received the prestigious Hopwood Award for poetry and had published his first volume of poems, *Heart-Shape in the Dust* (1940). After pursuing his MA at the University of Michigan, where he studied with W. H. Auden, who encouraged his technical innovations, Hayden began a twenty-three-year teaching career at Fisk University, returning to the University of Michigan to teach in 1969. His many publications include *The Lion and the Archer* (1948), *A Ballad of Remembrance* (1962), *Selected Poems* (1966), *Words in the Mourning Time* (1970), and the posthumous *Collected Poems* (1985). Appointed consultant in poetry to the Library of Congress (the full title is now poet laureate consultant in poetry) in 1976, Hayden was the first African American to occupy that office.

Born in Mount Sterling, Kentucky, in 1952, the son of an evangelical minister who served as a pastor in Redondo Beach, California, **Mark Jarman** graduated in 1974 from the University of California, Santa Cruz, where he studied with Raymond Carver. Two years later Jarman earned an MFA from the University of Iowa. A key figure in the formation of the "New Narrative" movement, he has championed the storytelling tradition of poetry in his critical study *The Secret of Poetry* (2001) and in a series of impressive, award-winning volumes that include *Tonight Is the Night of the Prom* (1974), *North Sea* (1978), *The Rote Walker* (1981), *Far and Away* (1985), *The Black Riviera* (1990), a verse novella, *Iris* (1992), *The Past from the Air* (1992), *Questions for Ecclesiastes* (1997), which won the Lenore Marshall Poetry Prize, and *Unholy Sonnets* (2000). He is a professor of English at Vanderbilt University. In "The Supremes," one of his best-known poems from *Far and Away,* Jarman revisits the Redondo Beach of his adolescence.

The author of more than twenty volumes of poetry, **Elizabeth Jennings** (1926–2001) was born in Lincolnshire and took honors in English at Oxford University, where she became loosely associated with writers belonging to a literary affiliation known as "The Movement," that included Kingsley Amis, Iris Murdoch, and Philip Larkin (see below). But she never gained the reputation in the United States that the others did. Her work is characterized by a colloquial use of traditional forms and her devout Catholicism is often apparent. Her first volume, *Poems* (1953), received the Somerset Maugham Award, the first of many awards she obtained throughout a prolific literary career. The volumes *Recoveries* (1964) and *The Mind Has Mountains* (1966) reflect on her breakdown and hospitalization in the early 1960s. *Collected Poems, 1953–1985* appeared in 1987; a new edition would be welcome, as she published steadily up until the end of her life.

John Keats (1795–1821) was born into a fairly prosperous family, though his father's humble origins would later make Keats the butt of Tory snobbery in the literary reviews. When Keats was eight his father died in a riding accident and then at the age of fourteen his mother died of tuberculosis. Falling under the care of a guardian with a more practical than poetic bent, Keats was apprenticed to a London surgeon to learn medicine, a trade he abandoned in 1817, when he published his first volume of poetry. Soon after losing his brother to tuberculosis in 1818, Keats experienced one of the most remarkable bursts of creativity in English literary history, writing many of his major poems. On December 30, 1816, perhaps dreaming of summer, Keats wrote "On the Grasshopper and Cricket" in response to a challenge from his friend Leigh Hunt, who simultaneously composed a sonnet on the same topic. A few months after his twenty-fifth birthday, Keats died in Rome of the family disease that had haunted him for years.

Yusef Komunyakaa, who has received numerous honors and awards, including a Pulitzer Prize for *Neon Vernacular* in 1994, the Ruth Lilly Poetry Prize in 2001, and a Bronze Star for service as a journalist in Vietnam, was born in Bogalusa, Louisiana, in 1947. His first book of poetry, *Dedications & Other Darkhorses,* appeared in 1977, and subsequent volumes include *Copacetic* (1984), *I Apologize for the Eyes in My Head* (1986), *Dien Cai Dau* (1988), *Magic City* (1992), *Thieves of Paradise* (1998), *Talking Dirty to the Gods* (2000), and *Pleasure Dome: New & Collected Poems, 1975–1999* (2001). He has written extensively on jazz and in 1999 was elected a chancellor of the Academy of American Poets. He lives in New York City and is a professor in the Council of Humanities and Creative Writing Program at Princeton University.

Stanley Kunitz was born into a Lithuanian immigrant family in Worcester, Massachusetts, in 1905. After graduating from Harvard in 1926, he continued on there to earn an MA and then took a publishing job in New York City. His first book of poetry, *Intellectual Things* (1930), received so little notice that he waited until after his World War II army service to publish his next volume, *Passport to War* (1944), which also failed to attract much attention. Kunitz's persistence, however, paid off, as his *Selected Poems* received the Pulitzer Prize in 1958. Since then, he has led a distinguished literary career as a poet, translator, critic, teacher, editor, and mentor, and has received numerous awards, including the Bollingen Prize, the Lenore Marshall Poetry Prize, Harvard's Centennial Medal, and the National Medal of the Arts. Appointed poet laureate in 2000, his later works include *Passing Through: The Later Poems, New and Selected* (1995), which won the National Book Award, and *The Collected Poems of Stanley Kunitz* (2000). He is chancellor emeritus of the Academy of American Poets.

Named after the Renaissance poet Sir Philip Sidney, **Philip Larkin** (1922–1985) was born in Coventry, Warwickshire, and entered Oxford in 1940, escaping conscription because of his terrible eyesight. At Oxford he became close friends with the novelist Kingsley Amis, and the two became influential members of a literary affiliation known as "The Movement." Reclusive and reluctant to lecture or give readings, Larkin worked most of his life as a librarian at the University of Hull. Each of his published volumes of poetry—among them *The North Ship* (1945), *The Less Deceived* (1955), *The Whitsun Weddings* (1964), and his final collection, *High Windows* (1974)—resonates with his remarkably understated wit and colloquial eloquence.

A book editor, writer, and artist in San Francisco, **Carolyn Miller** is the author of several volumes of poetry: a letterpress, limited-edition collection of *Constant Lover*—the poems are arranged by the seasons—was published in 2001 and *After Cocteau* followed a year later. Her work has appeared in many literary periodicals, including the *Georgia Review, Shenandoah,* the *Gettysburg Review,* and the *Southern Review.* She has received the James Boatwright III Award for Poetry from *Shenandoah* and the Rainmaker Award from *Zone 3.* In "Dark, Starry, Sticky Night: Missouri" she sensuously evokes the summers of her childhood.

Mary Oliver was born in 1935 in Maple Heights, Ohio. Her many books include *Why I Wake Early* (2004), *Winter Hours: Prose, Prose Poems, and Poems* (1999); *West Wind* (1997); *White Pine* (1994); *New and Selected Poems, Volume One* (1992), which won the National Book Award; *House of Light* (1990), the winner of the Christopher Award and the L. L. Winship/PEN New England Award; and *American Primitive* (1983), which won the Pulitzer Prize. She has also written *Rules for the Dance: A Handbook for Writing and Reading Metrical Verse* (1998); *Blue Pastures* (1995); and *A Poetry Handbook* (1994). She has received an American Academy of Arts and Letters Award, a Lannan Literary Award, and fellowships from the Guggenheim Foundation and the National Endowment for the Arts.

Marge Piercy was born in Detroit, Michigan, in 1936. After graduating from the University of Michigan, she earned an MA from Northwestern University. Her many books of poetry include *The Art of Blessing the Day: Poems with a Jewish Theme* (1999), *Early Grrrl: The Early Poems of Marge Piercy* (1999), *What Are Big Girls Made Of?* (1997), *Mars and Her Children* (1992), *Available Light* (1988), *Circles on the Water: Selected Poems of Marge Piercy* (1982), and *The Moon Is Always Female* (1980). She has written fifteen novels, including *Three Women* (1999), *City of Darkness, City of Light* (1996), *The Longings of Women* (1994), and *He, She and It* (1991). In 1998 she coauthored a novel, *Storm Tide,* with her husband, Ira Wood. She lives in Wellfleet, Massachusetts.

Called the "godfather of the beats," the poet, critic, and translator **Kenneth Rexroth** (1905–1982) was born in South Bend, Indiana, orphaned at the age of twelve, and spent his adolescence in Chicago, where—largely self-educated—he became immersed in a world of jazz, labor struggles, and anarchist politics, getting to know such radical figures as Emma Goldman, Eugene Debs, and Clarence Darrow. He moved to San Francisco in 1927, and as a conscientious objector during World War II worked to help Japanese Americans in detainment camps. Later, he was instrumental in shaping the city's cultural renaissance and creating the foundations for the beat movement of the 1950s and 1960s. In one of the wonderful anecdotes of this period, Rexroth is said to have opened a reading by asking the audience, "Well, what would you like tonight, sex, mysticism, or revolution?" "What's the difference?" a woman answered. In addition to many collections of critical essays, his major books of poetry include *In What Hour?* (1940), *The Phoenix and the Tortoise* (1944), *In Defense of the Earth* (1956), *The Complete Collected Shorter Poems* (1967), and *New Poems* (1974).

A prolific poet, novelist, and memoirist, the Belgium-born **Eleanore Marie (May) Sarton** (1912–1995) came to the United States with her parents at the age of four to escape the Wehrmacht invasion. She grew up in Cambridge, Massachusetts, and published her first poetry at the age of seventeen, when she also left home to join New York's Civic Repertory Theater. In 1933 she founded her own repertory theater in Hartford, Connecticut, but when that failed, she left acting and returned to writing. Her first collection, *Encounter in April,* appeared in 1937 and was followed by over a dozen more volumes of poetry, numerous novels, and a handful of autobiographies. She taught at Harvard and Wellesley before moving permanently to Maine in 1973. Her *Collected Poems* was published in 1993, shortly before she died of breast cancer.

Anne Sexton (1928–1974) was born in Newton, Massachusetts, and spent her entire life in the Boston vicinity. As a young woman she briefly modeled and—not possessing a college degree—studied poetry in adult-education workshops, where she met Maxine Kumin, who became a lifelong friend. Married at the age of twenty, Sexton went through years of therapy with occasional institutionalization after several devastating mental breakdowns in the mid-1950s, stark experiences that form the core of her first award-winning volume of poetry, *To Bedlam and Part Way Back* (1960). Her emotional stability again deteriorated after her divorce in 1973, and not long afterward she committed suicide.

Unlike most of the poets included here, **William Shakespeare** (1564–1616) received no prestigious awards and earned no degrees, but he nevertheless enjoyed financial success and thundering applause as a theatrical entrepreneur, an actor, and one of the most popular London playwrights of his time. The applause continues still and will undoubtedly never cease. Like the Beatles, who "discovered" rock and roll when the trend appeared to be over, Shakespeare saw his sonnet sequence published (without his consent) in 1609, long after such sequences were fashionable. By then he had already written nearly all of his major plays and was about to retire to his birthplace, Stratford-upon-Avon.

Born in 1963 in New York City, where he grew up in Bronx housing projects, **Reginald Shepherd** earned his BA from Bennington College and an MFA from both Brown University and the University of Iowa. He received the 1993 Associated Writing Programs' Award in Poetry for his first book, *Some Are Drowning,* and his second volume, *Angel, Interrupted,* was a finalist for the 1997 Lambda Literary Award. "Surface Effects in Summer Wind" appeared in his third book, *Wrong* (1999), which was widely praised: "All the ways," wrote the poet Mark Doty, "in which Reginald Shepherd is 'wrong' (not white, not straight, not apologetic, not believing in any easy way of making sense) fire these compelling poems—which brilliantly filter their urban, late twentieth century experience through the gorgeous diction of Marlowe and Hart Crane." Among other major awards, Shepherd has received a 1993 "Discovery"/*The Nation* award, grants from the National Endowment for the Arts, the Illinois Arts Council, and the Constance Saltonstall Foundation for the Arts. His fourth volume, *Otherhood,* was published in 2003.

A reader who would like to enjoy a perfect surrealistic literary experience could do no better than open the 1954 volume of *The Collected Poems of Wallace Stevens* and read the titles listed in the contents straight through as if they were the successive lines of a complete poem. Born in Reading, Pennsylvania, **Wallace Stevens** (1879–1955) attended Harvard and, after completing his law degree in New York, began a successful career as an insurance executive in Hartford, Connecticut, where he lived from 1916 until his death. His first book, *Harmonium* (1923), remains one of the most impressive first volumes of poetry in American literary history, although his critical acceptance came slowly. His other major volumes include *Ideas of Order* (1936), *The Man with the Blue Guitar* (1937), and *Parts of a World* (1942). He won both the Pulitzer Prize and the National Book Award for *The Collected Poems*. Although known for his many memorable winter landscape poems, he also wrote numerous celebrations of summer, such as "The House Was Quiet and the World Was Calm," which appeared in the volume *Transport to Summer* (1947).

Sharan Strange's first volume of poetry, *Ash,* was selected by Sonia Sanchez for the 2000 Barnard New Woman Poets Prize. One of seven children, Strange was raised in Orangeburg, South Carolina, and received her BA from Harvard University in 1981 and an MFA in poetry from Sarah Lawrence College. Her work has appeared in *The Best American Poetry* series as well as in many periodicals, including *Callaloo,* where she serves as an advisory and contributing editor. She has held positions as writer-in-residence at Fisk University, Spelman College, the University of California, and the California Institute of the Arts. Her poetry grows out of a deep sense of family and community relations: "I'm really preoccupied," she says, "with examining the family dynamic, what we can recollect, and what of the past we can reclaim and understand." She currently teaches poetry and creative writing in the English department of Spelman College.

A tall, rugged man who exerted a powerful physical presence, **Alfred Lord Tennyson** (1809–1892) grew up one of twelve children in a Lincolnshire parsonage described by the scholar George H. Ford as more broodingly Faulknerian than straitlaced Victorian. He learned classics from his father, began versifying early (a six-thousand-line epic at twelve), and published his first volume anonymously in 1827 just before he entered Trinity College, Cambridge, where he impressed both teachers and fellow students with the sonorous skills evident in *Poems, Chiefly Lyrical* (1830). After his father's death a year later, he left Cambridge and returned home to help his financially distressed family. Tennyson emotionally rebounded from his impoverished situation, the hostile reviews of his next book, the sudden death of his closest friend, and a prolonged postponement of marriage to publish his two-volume *Poems* in 1842 and then, still in debt and despair, one of his major books, *In Memoriam,* in 1850. After being named poet laureate later that year, Tennyson's reputation—and his prosperity—soared, and with such best-selling volumes as the Arthurian series *Idylls of the King* (first volume published in 1859) he increasingly became "the voice of his age," acquiring unprecedented popular success along with a peerage in 1884. Addressed to his wife, Emily, "June Bracken and Heather" served as the dedication to his last volume of poetry.

Few modern poets can match the rhetorical power of **Dylan Thomas** (1914–1953), whose rhapsodic readings brought him considerable fame in both England and the United States during the late 1940s and early 1950s. Thomas took the spoken word to new levels, but his sensational and well-attended performances would also prove fatal: he died suddenly after an alcohol binge following a New York City reading. Thomas was born in Swansea, Wales, and throughout his career his poetry retained its Welsh accent. He published his first volume of poetry, *18 Poems,* in 1934, a year before he settled in London, where he perfected his delivery skills as a broadcaster and writer for the BBC. With such later volumes as *Death and Entrances* (1946) and *Collected Poems* (1952), he convinced skeptical critics that a deep poetic talent lay indeed behind the theatrics. Besides poetry, children's tales, and several remarkable radio plays, Thomas also published a popular collection of autobiographical stories, *A Portrait of the Artist as a Young Dog* (1940). His well-known poem "Fern Hill" commemorates the summer vacations he spent as a child on an aunt's farm in the Welsh countryside.

Like Ralph Waldo Emerson, his friend and far more successful Concord neighbor, **Henry David Thoreau** (1817–1862) is better known for his prose than his poetry. After working his way through Harvard, Thoreau returned to Concord—he was the only one of the famed Concord literary group who was a native—where he unhappily taught school and tutored before joining the Emerson household as a handyman. On July 4, 1845, Thoreau undertook what would become one of America's legendary journeys, when he made the short trek from his home and built a small cabin on Emerson's land adjoining Walden Pond. From that experiment in living would come two powerful travel books: *A Week on the Concord and Merrimack Rivers* (1849), the book he had gone into seclusion to write, and his masterpiece, *Walden; or, Life in the Woods* (1854), the book that meticulously grew out of the notes and observations he made during his two years at Walden Pond. Neither of these books made any serious literary impact at the time, nor did the subsequent posthumously published travel narratives, *The Maine Woods* (1864) and *Cape Cod* (1865). Most of his meditative and political essays—as well as his remarkable journals and poetry—remained uncollected until years after his death from tuberculosis at age forty-four.

Derek Walcott was born into a racially and ethnically mixed family on the island of St. Lucia in the British West Indies in 1930. After graduating from the University of the West Indies in Jamaica in 1953, he moved to Trinidad, where he became deeply involved in theater, which he continued to study in the United States on a Rockefeller Foundation fellowship in 1957. With the publication in London of his fourth book, *In a Green Night* (1962), his career as a major poet was launched, and his international reputation as a poet of national and cultural estrangement grew with such volumes as *The Castaway* (1965), *The Gulf* (1970), *Another Life* (1973), *Sea Grapes* (1976), and *The Star-Apple Kingdom* (1979). In 1981, the year he published *The Fortunate Traveller,* he received a MacArthur Fellowship and joined the creative writing department at Boston University. The author of many award-winning plays and an accomplished artist, Walcott received the Nobel Prize in literature in 1992. His *Collected Poems* appeared in 1986 and later works include *The Bounty* (1997) and *Tiepolo's Hound* (2000).

Walt Whitman (1819–1892) is America's national poet, the single voice that most fully represents the American experience. *Leaves of Grass*, the volume he labored, fussed, and fought over from the first privately printed edition in 1855 until the "deathbed edition" of 1892, remains the most influential work of poetry in American literary history. Born into a working-class Long Island, New York, family, Whitman grew up as a Quaker in Brooklyn, dropping out of school at eleven to find a trade. Like Benjamin Franklin and Mark Twain, he learned printing, a skill that landed him several newspaper positions as a reporter and editorial writer. When the 1882 edition of *Leaves of Grass* was suppressed in Boston, the publicity helped the volume earn its best sales ever, and Whitman was able to buy a small house in Camden, New Jersey, where he modestly entertained distinguished visitors from all over the world and cultivated the many myths that began flourishing about him well before his death. "July Afternoon by the Pond" is one of the many prose lyrics from his journal *Specimen Days* (1882).

Verbally polished until they shine, **Richard Wilbur**'s poems have served as models of the poet's craft ever since *The Beautiful Changes and Other Poems* appeared in 1947. One would be hard-pressed to find a reputable textbook on the art of poetry that did not include examples of Wilbur's disciplined and exemplary work. Born in New York City in 1921, Wilbur was educated at Amherst College (where he studied with Robert Frost) and Harvard University. America's poet laureate in 1987, Wilbur won the Pulitzer Prize in 1989 for his *New and Collected Poems*. He has taught for many years at Wesleyan University and is also well known for his highly acclaimed translations of Molière. Wilbur received the Wallace Stevens Award in 2003.

Born in Brunswick, Maine, in 1930, **Robley Wilson** grew up in a New England Unitarian environment, where he gained the religious perspective that has informed his writing. He graduated from Bowdoin College in 1957, earning an MFA the following year from the University of Iowa. Although he began writing poems and stories as early as high school, he did not publish his first book, *The Pleasures of Manhood* (1977), until he was forty-seven. Praised for his accomplishments in both fiction and poetry, his other short story collections include *Living Alone* (1978), *Dancing for Men* (1983), *Terrible Kisses* (1989), and *The Book of Lost Fathers* (2001). His volumes of poetry, such as *Kingdoms of the Ordinary* (1987), *A Pleasure Tree* (1990), *A Walk through the Human Heart* (1996), and *Everything Paid For* (1999), have received several prestigious awards. His first novel, *The Victim's Daughter,* appeared in 1991, and another, *Splendid Omens,* in 2004. In 1963 Wilson began teaching at the University of Northern Iowa, where for thirty-one years he edited the *North American Review,* America's oldest literary journal. He now lives in Florida.

For several decades (**Arthur**) **Yvor Winters** (1900–1968) was one of America's most prominent critics and poets. Born in Chicago and raised in New Mexico, Winters earned his BA and MA from the University of Colorado and his doctorate from Stanford, where he taught for many years; his students included the poets Thom Gunn and Robert Pinsky. Winters published poetry before he graduated from college, *The Immobile Wind* appearing in 1921, and he is the author of many subsequent volumes, including The *Bare Hills* (1927), *The Proof* (1930), *The Giant Weapon* (1943), and *Collected Poems* (1960), which received the Bollingen Prize. Best known today for his criticism, which emphasizes the importance of rationality and morality in literature, Winters waged a battle against romantic obscurantism in such books as *Primitivism and Decadence* (1937), *Maule's Curse* (1938), and *The Anatomy of Nonsense* (1943), which are all collected in *In Defense of Reason* (1947). He published *The Function of Criticism* in 1957.

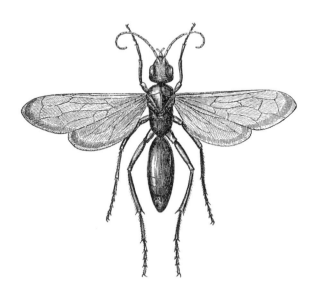

CREDITS

A. R. AMMONS
"Mid-August" from *Collected Poems, 1951–1971* by A. R. Ammons. Copyright © 1972 by A. R. Ammons. Used by permission of W. W. Norton & Company, Inc.

JOHN ASHBERY
"Summer" from *A Double Dream of Spring*. Copyright © 1970, 1969, 1968, 1967, 1966 by John Ashbery. Reprinted by permission of Georges Borchardt, Inc., for the author.

LOUISE BOGAN
"Dark Summer" from *The Blue Estuaries: Poems 1923–1968* by Louise Bogan. Copyright © 1968 by Louise Bogan and renewed 1996 by Ruth Limmer. Reprinted by permission of Farrar, Straus and Giroux, LLC.

RICHARD EBERHART
"A Loon Call" from *Collected Poems 1930–1986* by Richard Eberhart, copyright © 1960, 1976, 1987 by Richard Eberhart. Used by permission of Oxford University Press, Inc.

LOUISE GLÜCK
"Solstice" from *The Seven Ages* by Louise Glück. Copyright © 2001 by Louise Glück. Reprinted by permission of HarperCollins Publishers Inc.

KERRY HARDIE
"Sleep in Summer" from *The Sky Didn't Fall* by Kerry Hardie. Copyright © 2003 by Kerry Hardie. Reprinted by kind permission of the author and The Gallery Press, Loughcrew, Oldcastle, County Meath, Ireland.

ROBERT HAYDEN
"Summertime and the Living . . ." from *Collected Poems of Robert Hayden* by Robert Hayden, edited by Frederick Glaysher. Copyright © 1985 by Emma Hayden. Used by permission of Liveright Publishing Corporation.

MARK JARMAN
Reprinted from *Far and Away*: "The Supremes" by permission of Carnegie Mellon University Press, copyright © 1985 by Mark Jarman.

YUSEF KOMUNYAKAA
"Happiness" from *Pleasure Dome: New and Selected Poems*, © 2001 by Yusef Komun-

yakaa and reprinted by permission of Wesleyan University Press. All rights reserved.

STANLEY KUNITZ
"End of the Summer" from *The Collected Poems* by Stanley Kunitz. Copyright © 2000 by Stanley Kunitz. Used by permission of W. W. Norton & Company, Inc.

PHILIP LARKIN
"Mother, Summer, I" from *Collected Poems* by Philip Larkin. Copyright © 1988, 1989 by the Estate of Philip Larkin. Reprinted by permission of Farrar, Straus and Giroux, LLC.

CAROLYN MILLER
"Dark, Starry, Sticky Night: Missouri" by Carolyn Miller originally appeared in *The Chattahoochee Review,* Spring, 2002. Reprinted by permission of *The Chattahoochee Review.*

MARY OLIVER
"While I Am Writing a Poem to Celebrate Summer, the Meadowlark Begins to Sing" from *Owls and Other Fantasies* by Mary Oliver © 2003 by Mary Oliver. Reprinted by permission of Beacon Press and the author. All rights reserved.

MARGE PIERCY
"Very late July" from *Stone, Paper, Knife* by Marge Piercy, copyright © 1983 by Marge Piercy. Used by permission of Alfred A. Knopf, a division of Random House, Inc.

KENNETH REXROTH
"Gic to Har" by Kenneth Rexroth, from *Collected Shorter Poems.* Copyright © 1966 by Kenneth Rexroth. Reprinted by permission of New Directions Publishing Corporation.

MAY SARTON
"Summer Music" from *Collected Poems 1930–1993* by May Sarton. Copyright © 1993, 1988, 1984, 1980, 1974 by May Sarton. Used by permission of W. W. Norton & Company, Inc.

ANNE SEXTON
"The Kite" from *To Bedlam and Part Way Back* by Anne Sexton. Copyright © 1960 by Anne Sexton, renewed 1988 by Linda G. Sexton. Reprinted by permission of Houghton Mifflin Company. All rights reserved.

REGINALD SHEPHERD
"Surface Effects in Summer Wind" by Reginald Shepherd originally appeared in *The Virginia Quarterly Review,* Winter 1999. Reprinted by permission of *The Virginia Quarterly Review.*

WALLACE STEVENS
"The House Was Quiet and the World Was Calm" from *The Collected Poems of Wallace Stevens* by Wallace Stevens, copyright © 1954 by Wallace Stevens and renewed 1982 by Holly Stevens. Used by permission of Alfred A. Knopf, a division of Random House, Inc.

SHARAN STRANGE
Strange, Sharan. Childhood. Callaloo 16:1 (1993), 15. © Charles H. Rowell. Reprinted with permission of The Johns Hopkins University Press.

DYLAN THOMAS
"Fern Hill" by Dylan Thomas, from *The Poems of Dylan Thomas.* Copyright © 1945 by The Trustees for the Copyrights of Dylan Thomas. Reprinted by permission of New Directions Publishing Corporation.

DEREK WALCOTT
"Bleecker Street, Summer" from *Collected Poems: 1948–1984* by Derek Walcott. Copyright © 1986 by Derek Walcott. Reprinted by permission of Farrar, Straus and Giroux, LLC.

RICHARD WILBUR
"My Father Paints the Summer" from *The Beautiful Changes and Other Poems,* copyright © 1947 and renewed 1975 by Richard Wilbur, reprinted by permission of Harcourt, Inc.

"Exeunt" from *Things of This World,* copyright © 1952 and renewed 1980 by Richard Wilbur, reprinted by permission of Harcourt, Inc.

ROBLEY WILSON
"In summer, nothing happens" originally appeared in *The New Criterion,* December 1999. It is reprinted here by permission of the author.

YVOR WINTERS
"Summer Noon, 1941" by Yvor Winters, from *The Selected Poems of Yvor Winters.* Reprinted with the permission of Swallow Press/Ohio University Press, Athens, Ohio.

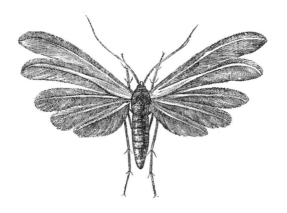